PENGUIN BOOKS

THE SOBBING SCHOOL

Joshua Bennett received his PhD in English from Princeton University. He is currently a member of the Society of Fellows at Harvard University, and has received fellowships from the Callaloo Creative Writing Workshop, the Josephine de Karman Fellowship Trust, the Hurston/Wright Foundation, and the Ford Foundation. His poems have been published or are forthcoming in *Beloit Poetry Journal*, *Callaloo*, *The Kenyon Review*, and *New England Review*. Bennett tours nationally and internationally as a performance artist and has recited his original work at the Sundance Film Festival, the NAACP Image Awards, and President Obama's Evening of Poetry, Music, and the Spoken Word at the White House. He lives in New York City.

THE NATIONAL POETRY SERIES

The National Poetry Series was established in 1978 to ensure the publication of five collections of poetry annually through five participating publishers. Publication is funded annually by the Lannan Foundation; Amazon Literary Partnership; Barnes & Noble; the Poetry Foundation; the PG Family Foundation; and the Betsy Community Fund; Joan Bingham, Mariana Cook, Stephen Graham, Juliet Lea Hillman Simonds, William Kistler, Jeffrey Ravetch, Laura Baudo Sillerman, and Margaret Thornton. For a complete listing of generous contributors to the National Poetry Series, please visit www.nationalpoetryseries.org.

2015 COMPETITION WINNERS

Not on the Last Day, But on the Very Last, by Justin Boening
of Iowa City, IA
Chosen by Wayne Miller, to be published by Milkweed Editions

The Wug Test, by Jennifer Kronovet of New York, NY
Chosen by Eliza Griswold, to be published by Ecco

Scriptorium, by Melissa Range of Appleton, WI
Chosen by Tracy K. Smith, to be published by Beacon Press

Trébuchet, by Danniel Schoonebeek of Brooklyn, NY
Chosen by Kevin Prufer, to be published by
University of Georgia Press

The Sobbing School, by Joshua Bennett of New York, NY
Chosen by Eugene Gloria, to be published by Penguin Books

THE SOBBING SCHOOL

JOSHUA BENNETT

PENGUIN BOOKS

PENGUIN BOOKS

An imprint of Penguin Random House LLC
375 Hudson Street
New York, New York 10014
penguin.com

LIBRARY OF CONGRESS CATALOGING-IN-PUBLICATION DATA
Names: Bennett, Joshua (Poet)
Title: The sobbing school / Joshua Bennett.
Description: New York, New York : Penguin Books, 2016. | Series: National poetry series
Identifiers: LCCN 2016020931 (print) | LCCN 2016025326 (ebook) |
ISBN 9780143111863 (paperback) | ISBN 9781101993101 (ebook)
Subjects: | BISAC: POETRY / American / General. | POETRY /
American / African American.
Classification: LCC PS3602.E664483 A6 2016 (print) | LCC PS3602.E664483 (ebook) |
DDC 811/.6—dc23
LC record available at https://lccn.loc.gov/2016020931

Printed in the United States of America
1   3   5   7   9   10   8   6   4   2

Set in Adobe Caslon Pro
Designed by Ginger Legato

For my father & mother, who dreamt of other worlds

I do not belong to the sobbing school of Negrohood who hold that nature somehow has given them a lowdown dirty deal and whose feelings are all hurt about it. . . . No, I do not weep at the world—I am too busy sharpening my oyster knife.

—ZORA NEALE HURSTON

ACKNOWLEDGMENTS

I would like to thank the following journals for publishing poems featured in this book:

Anti-: "12 absolutely true facts about Richard Wright"

Backbone: "In Defense of Henry Box Brown"

Beloit Poetry Journal: "Love Poem Ending with Typewriters" and "On Blueness"

Blackbird: "On Flesh," "Samson Reconsiders," and "VCR&B"

Callaloo: "First Date" and "Yoke"

The Collagist: "Clench" and "home force: presumption of death"

Connotation Press: "Black History, abridged"

CURA: "Fade"

Drunken Boat: "Didn't Old Pharaoh Get Lost in the Red Sea: theorizing amnesia in Afro-diasporic maritime literature"

Fjords Review: "Anthropophobia"

The Kenyon Review: "Praise song for the table in the cafeteria where all the black boys sat together during A Block, laughing too loudly" and "X"

Kweli: "Self-Portrait as *Periplaneta Americana*"

Magma: "Teacher's Aide"

New England Review: "Aubade with Insomnia" and "The Sobbing School"

Obsidian: "Whenever Hemingway Hums *Nigger*"

Pinwheel: "On Stupidity," "Taxonomy," and "Tenacious Elegy: Insurgent Life in the Era of Trial by Gunfire with a Line from Sylvia Wynter"

Smartish Pace: "Fresh"

Storyscape: "The Order of Things"

Tupelo Quarterly: "Still Life with First Best Friend"

Vinyl: "Invocation"

Wave Composition: "On Extinction" and "Praise House"

Word Riot: "Theodicy"

I cannot imagine this book's entry into the world of the living without the insight and unfettered imagination of Imani Perry, Salamishah Tillet, Charles Rowell, Gregory Pardlo, Josef Sorett, Camille Dungy, Terrance Hayes, Kyle Dargan, Ashon Crawley, Jesse McCarthy, and the entirety of the Black Studies Colloquium at Columbia University. Deepest gratitude to Phillip B. Williams for his singular editorial acuity, and Eugene Gloria for believing in the vision I set out to elaborate herein. Special thanks to Paul Slovak for his patience and trust. Thank you to the members of the Mourners Bench—Jamall Calloway, Jeremy Scott Vinson, and Wesley Morris—for the countless hours spent reading, laughing, and living on in spite of. Thank you to Thiahera Nurse for the series of poetry exchanges that led to the completion of this manuscript, as well as for being the sort of collaborator and friend that makes this work a joyous occasion. Thank you to the *Kinfolks* editorial board: Jerriod Avant, Desiree Bailey, Lauren Yates, Safia Elhillo, Nate Marshall, Sean DesVignes, and Aziza Barnes for their commitment to the cultivation, rigorous study, and unrelenting celebration of black expressive cultures. Thank you to my Strivers Row family past and present: Alysia Harris, Carvens Lissaint, Miles Hodges, Zora Howard, and every single person that has ever come out to one of our shows. Devin, you already know. Marcus, thank you for always holding me accountable to the people and places I care about most. Thank you, Miles, my beautiful, brilliant nephew, for always reminding me that another world is on its way. And finally, dearest Toya, thank you for all you have done to help me build a kind of life from words given to the air; this book would not exist without your tutelage, your valor, your steadfast love.

CONTENTS

THE SOBBING SCHOOL

Not every trauma has a price
point. You & I are special
that way. No doubt, there is good
money to be made in the rehearsal of
a father's rage, an empty crate,
whatever instrument ushered us into
lives of impure repetition. Years on
end, you replayed your infamous
escape for hundreds
of tearful devoted, sold out
shows an ocean away from the place
that made you possible, made you
parcel, uncommon contraband carried
over amber ululations of grain
& grass & filthy hands:
white, black, unwitting all the same.
If they had only known the weight
of what passed before them.
The wait you waded through.
Twenty-seven hours spent inside
a three-by-two-foot jail of splinter & rust. I too
have signed over the rights to all my
best wounds. I know the stage
is a leviathan with no proper name
to curtail its breadth. I know
the respectable man enjoys a dark
body best when it comes with a good
cry thrown in. I know all the code
words, Henry. Why you nicknamed
the violence. Why all your nightmares
end in vermilion.

Please, pardon my obsession
with endings. I was born of two Baptists,
one backslidden though no less
fervent when it came to the law,
the cross, the grain of me
& my sister's hair. I was born
nonwhite in the 1980s,
arrived in the wake of four girls
slumped against a project wall
resembling a long ellipsis, *heron*
(my father's preferred pronunciation)
having coaxed their heads
into solemn agreement.

Mama knew three of the dying
personally, but maybe this isn't about her,
so much as how this scene became a part
of our extended family, its argument
clear as a bullet's signature: to live
in this flesh is to worship agility,
to call death by its government name.

The woman across the table from me is scared
to raise her son, fears he will be killed
by police, says this outright, over soup,
expecting nothing.

My first thought is of the landscape.
For a moment, all I can see is flat green oblivion,
unchecked flora where fourth graders

once sped across the open. In 1896,
Frederick Hoffman claimed every Negro
in the U.S. would be dead by the year
of my younger brother's birth. To his credit,
Hoffman dreamt of neither badge nor bullet,
but dysentery, tuberculosis, killers
we could not touch or beg for clemency.

Hence, when I consider extinction,
I do not think of sad men with guns,
or Hoffman standing by the chalkboard
in his office, discerning algorithms
for the dead, but of our refusal,
how my mother, without stopping

even to write a poem about it,
woke up that day,
& this morning again.

Pray for flame
with the diligence of a saint,
scarlet tongues of light sharp enough

to cut bone & soul just the same.
My parents praise a vengeful God.
Son of all three, what else did I inherit

but this commitment to the scales?
The killer woke up today.
Probably ate scrambled eggs

for breakfast, brushed his teeth
three times or fewer, walked
in soft slippers through the living

room, checked the mail
while a child decomposed underground,
held still beneath the bloodless weight

of the law. Baldwin sang *The Fire Next Time*
in 1963 & we are living in the wake
of his impossible love. I too dream

of such heat. I yearn for nothing
if not equilibrium, a means to honor
how elders taught me to pray:

Lord, if you be
at all, be
a blade.

YOKE

1

consider the yoke.   its violent geometry.

how wood and metal

            blur every border.

grandpa Earl is tilling tobacco in the heavy dark,

cuffed by the neck to a nameless mule.

when he meets Lena, he will propose on the spot.

repent of the land. head north to hunt for a clean start.

            tobacco season came and fled.

1933 paused to catch its breath

            and grandpa was gone.

started a second family right down the block. thought it providence.

2

my mother stays for the sake of premise, a promise made in the wake

of my sister's birth. she loves us despite him. to spite him.

she cannot leave any more than she can unlearn the shape of our mouths.

what does it mean to be wholly for another? to count your seed as both anchor

and anima?

3

bulletproof glass turned my older brother into a prime number.
stuffed his libretto in a cage. corrections: as if he were an essay of
bone. dad was wrong. the belt's leather cadence is all my brother
and I share, all that binds us across age and the irreverence of steel.

as cormorant. as crow. as colon. as comma.
as coma. as shadow. as shade. as show.
as collards. as collection plate. as play cousin.
as dozens. as sea. as depth where light
don't dare tread. as treason. as gun. as gullet.
as gully. as ghetto came to be named.
as Cain. as antonym. as animal ontology.
as analogy always. as antimatter.
as bullet's best bet. as best friend. as bobby
pin. as Bobby Brown. as *brown crayons*
color everything in this house. as the inside
of a nap. as Mama's naps. as the hot comb
she used to lay them down like a burden.
as burden. as burial. as breath. as break beat.
as breaking: as anything that burns.

DIDN'T OLD PHARAOH GET LOST IN THE RED SEA: THEORIZING AMNESIA IN AFRO-DIASPORIC MARITIME LITERATURE

Keywords: absence, being-for-another, undertow, thalassophobia, phantom limb

Abstract:

Though there has certainly been a recent wave of scholarship in the field of hydropoetics that attends to the necessarily fraught relationship between writers of the African diaspora and their encounters with the sea, many of which are watermarked by the serrated memory of the Middle Passage and its afterlife, what has heretofore been left largely undertheorized are the ways in which these very same writers might encounter the sea as a trick mirror against which they are able to craft new worlds out of black, wet infinity, like Elohim in Genesis 1 or a child in a darkroom. Thus, this poem is interested in using the moment the speaker looks into the sea for the first time on a family trip to Antigua, thousands of miles away from the unknowable depth of his block, which is its own kind of benthos, as a springboard for considering what it means to never be able to regain what is lost (even a name or less heavy tongue) and what that sort of truancy can make of a seven-year-old who, even then, could not shake the feeling that his legs were not his own.

THEODICY

for Renisha McBride

When yet another one of your kin falls,
you question God's wingspan, the architecture
of mercy. It is Friday morning, & despair
is the only law

left intact. No one knows how to stop
the bleeding. This many black bodies deep,
the synonymy between ropes & gunfire is lost
on no one, you assume. You assumed, brother,

that this was your solitary cross, the only anguish
your daughter might actually be spared: the bull's-eye,
its glare, this hunt you know better than any other algorithm:
subtraction by bullet, our daily negation, how ageless it is,

the laughter too, yes, the grisly surprise
of every birthday past the age of 18,
the music we have yet to invent
for mourning this specific.

Detroit wails in the wake of a shotgun blast
& you do not know how to write
what you can't imagine the end of.
Why don't we grieve for women,

for girls, the same way we do
our men, our vanishing boys?
Perhaps it is this body, ever mutable
in its danger, always shifting between target

& terror that demands too much
recognition, this history of sons swinging
& drowned & cut up & caged
that elides revision, leaves no space

for other grief. Genuflected by disbelief,
you spend entire nights alone,
folded into the shape of a mouth,
cursing the limits of strength.

My mother claims that I began to run
long before I walked or spoke
or wore shoes & she too
is not a man that she should lie.
Thus, if we are willing
to count this creation myth
as admissible evidence, what
conclusions can be drawn
about my own penchant
for leaving, all this slow heat
in my blood, propelling me
like a denouement toward the door?

In seventh grade, Anthony tells me to "run" my pockets & I am only vaguely familiar with the term. His fists, like this new word for truancy, are intruders, thieves come to break the world in half. Final inventory: three dimes & a pack of Winterfresh I bought that morning, my mint-condition, holographic Ken Griffey Jr. rookie card now the property of another boy, his smile a firing squad I will face every day for the next nine weeks. I hate Anthony. Not only for the theft itself, his crime against civility, but for the shame I will wear like a brother's shirt for years to come, replaying this scene over & over. In the final edits, I surprise the brigand with a left hook to the jaw for good measure, hands still empty apart from a righteous rage at the helm of each wrist, as if Ahab in the storm, praying the bolt strike true & make him holy.

So I have this dream, right? Where it's the first few minutes before whichever apocalypse option is first to leap off the shelf—

Option A: The boys in blue kill every sick, sad one of us sans myself in a mad dash for department honors.

Option B: The sky cracks open like a green bottle in the freezer, which lays the groundwork for God's volcanic rage to turn the entire grid to cinders, & I'm just standing there, right, surveying the scene like some bizarre homage to Lewis & Clark, & look up, full of mourning, ignoring every cockroach in earshot singing Motown with scraps of human bone in their mouths, belt out, *"Well dammit fellas the fall was hard & swift as wrath, but great while it lasted, yeah? We had a nice little run there, didn't we?"*

STILL LIFE WITH FIRST BEST FRIEND

after Jericho Brown

Danny in the scrum
& his hands are meadowlarks,
their fulvous ascent. Danny after
the fact. Danny listening to you weep,
quiet as this umpteenth L must be
kept. Danny does what all best
friends who growth-spurt first must do.
Danny defends. Danny deflects
classroom heat, the jokes that land like lash
& linger. Danny suspended like twice.
Danny can't safeguard in absentia. Danny talks
about his daddy same way you do yours
when yours goes phantom. Danny ethics.
Danny don't go missing. Danny forged in flame.
Danny igneous. Danny obsidian. Danny covert
nerd on black ops mission. Danny Magic cards.
Danny Charizard. Danny still blacker than you
depending on that day's definition.
Danny Bigger Thomas & Big Bird & Big Pun
in the same bookcase. Danny all-inclusive
literary tradition. Danny claims your block,
its very bricks as kin: you tell him
duty is a dead idea. Danny won't listen.
Danny principles. Early twenties you talk tough
& Danny gets defensive. You do school, J.
Someone starts problems out here, you call me.
That's my business. Danny stabbed twice & shot once
& still smooth as a piston. Danny illegible.
Danny family. Nobody else checks in on Dad
when you forget to miss him.

FADE

My childhood fade was so high and well moisturized
I would often tell passersby that it was a black box built
by rogue scientists in case anything in my body
ever crashed again and they needed access to backup
recordings of all my best and most important dreams:

Y'all remember when Wahid fought Jason back
in 4th grade because Jason kept making
all those jokes about Wahid's little brother
riding the small bus and this man Jason caught
the FADE in front of our entire school?
Y'all remember that? How Wahid just
stood there after, staring at the crater
Jason left in the grass? Like he forgot something?

it feels less like the southpaw cross
your friends foretold, more like fresh talon
sailing across the eye's tundra.

your neck snaps
back: a black
bow in winter, a black boy in summer.
you register the wound. halfway down the page,
waist-deep in *The Sun Also Rises*, you admonish
your twenty-first-century fragility. gentle theorist,

your life's work depends on mastering men
like this, on surviving
that which shames the tongue's lust
of utterance, demands:
just look at this
and try not to hate
what you can't make
bleed.

My father showed up to school that day dressed up
as a man with a son with a rage problem; that is, a boy
whom violence—as if rumor, fresh from out of town

—followed everywhere. Ms. Hollinger never mentioned
the more practical elements of this ongoing conflict,
that I fought the other students because I liked my blood

very much & wanted to keep all of it inside of my body
once the playground went feral, as it was wont to do.
From his first day on the new job, my father

would bribe the bullies as only a Casanova of his stature
could, butterscotches & dirty jokes quelling all prior conflict.
The shift was immediate. Now baptized in the flame

of an older man's beauty, the war on the wise guy
was no more: a cease-fire forged by sheer esteem,
the stuff of corner-store science fiction it was,

this lovely Marine standing watch, half smile
drawing both teachers & seventh-grade girls
to him like lightning to a god of gold.

PRAISE SONG FOR THE TABLE IN THE CAFETERIA WHERE ALL THE BLACK BOYS SAT TOGETHER DURING A BLOCK, LAUGHING TOO LOUDLY

> *What is this nonpower at the heart of power?*
> —JACQUES DERRIDA

Thomas was a riot. By which I mean funny
to the point you thought he practiced the same
set of jokes on the bus each morning

with the sole intention of ruining AP Bio,
but also as a gesture toward the chaos
he brought with him when he entered

the room, what his presence stole free in us.
When he walked by, white girls would flicker
their eyes at him like golden apertures, as if

they were trying to copyright his splendor,
or keep his swagger as an exhibit in a museum.
Quiet as it's kept, the combination of me & Thomas

& Jeremy & Devin & Eddie was the most color
our school had ever let through its doors
in a single year, our collective body both

a kind of shame & a pretty sweet school record
all by itself. All we had was A Block's release:
Thomas clowning everyone's clearance-rack running

shoes & lack of game; Devin's impromptu raps;
Eddie's impressions; & Jeremy, silent as a marble,
speaking only when he had a gem of a dagger

to drop like a dead bird in the desert, like the day
he called Thomas *a corny-ass rich boy*
& how from then on I could think of nothing

but the force of the slur as it sailed across
our plates, how selfish it was of Jeremy
to kill the vibe that way. I mean, really,

what's a biography worth
if your boys won't let it stretch?
Who in their right mind would want us,

our threadbare lives, without a little legend
to sweeten the frame?
What mattered the miles
between The Hood, its protean

borders, & our actual homes, or the first times
that never happened, or the nicknames
no one called us in real life,

when such warm fiction was shared
among this huddle of strangers
made lifelong friends

by a Scantron's omniscience,
by our careful parents & their justifiable
fear of the world?

IN DEFENSE OF PASSING

Most of us call it cloaking,
though the academic
term for the practice slides

just as smoothly off
a teenager's tongue:
holographic deracination.

Within days of wide-scale release,
the *Times* will hail this device, its
attendant social phenomena

as triumphs of modern technology,
inevitable advance given the speed
of post-racial desire,

how expensive it is
to purge the murk
from an infant's skin

by most other means.
The machine's inventor
will make no such claims.

A plainspoken woman, she was.
Stanford grad, white as a lab coat.
Cited her time overseas

as primary inspiration;
all the suffering she'd seen
caste cause. The device came

to her in a lucid dream, this silver ellipse
small enough to wear on the wrist
or lapel. With just one touch

any future you choose could be
yours. Soft, false flesh, draped
like a new lover over your body

& just as clumsily until you work out
the rhythm of it, the slang,
how to maneuver this

cold glass suit, light as it is.
Protest faded in days.
Sky-high pricing kept the cloaks

an upper-class concern for months, years
before poor folks got ahold
of any prototype worth the worry.

Once they did, you would think
they had stolen something worth more
than a date with the quarterback,

or a job interview. You would think
they had killed someone important,
or blown up the moon, the way cops

flooded the slums, clubs in hand,
beating the color off of them.

Trust, it was not so much that I thought the icon of Michael Jordan's smooth, triangular flight on the back of my first cousin's new shoes a proof of God, but rather that I likewise yearned for glory & honor. And so, after thirteen years of living at the lower end of the freshness spectrum, I figured there was no better way to spend a first check: white and red Retro III's with a triple-XL tall tee to match. Ecko jeans. Size 7⅝ Oakland A's fitted cap, New Era sticker above the brim shining like a Spanish doubloon. So fly, later that night I would stroll into the party slow as water shifting phase, bathed in strobe light, unfazed as every yet-uncoupled senior-class girl swooned without hesitation or shame, their glances cast like fishermen's nets through the air above the dance floor, giving musculature to the darkness.

◆

The first time I saw a black patent leather shoe fly across the living room, I knew Mama was nothing to be fooled with, though the lesson did not last long. Up to my senior year at the prep school she spent all the extra cash she hid from Dad on, I was wild as any brown boy with half a head of sense could be, slamming doors and sneaking through windows once the streetlights were already warm. It would be another year before I found the Beretta, or the spare bullets—which, back then, I took to be little more than the broken steel fingers of an elaborate necklace strewn, as if rock salt, throughout the dresser drawer. Let me try this again. Once, my mother gave her life to three great loves: Jehovah, travel, geraniums by the porch. These are not arranged in any meaningful order, depending on what your last great claim would be given the grace of a window in which to speak before it all goes dim. It is only a list. Hear me.

My mother, South Bronx–born, state-sponsored gun for hire, threw a shoe across a packed room and hit no one. Not even the boy she bore and taught to walk, now a foot taller than the man she named him after, yelling for minutes on end at no one but her, whom he loves, whom he would give all the blood in his body for.

after e.e.

When Richard Wright was five years old he torched
his mama's living room curtains just to see cinder blacken
his father's hands like the insides of a loganberry pie.

Richard Wright was a steel-driving man. Richard Wright
could fly. Richard Wright wrote his last book about lice
& magnolia blossoms & it went viral in Mississippi.

Richard Wright had a zoologist twin sister named Giovanna.
Sadly, her work did not outlive her. Richard Wright outlived
every talking horse he ever met. Richard Wright loved

to hoop. Reputable sources swear he was trash with his left.
Richard Wright was born in a hornet's nest. In 1975,
he beat Earl "The Pearl" Monroe in a game of H-O-R-S-E.

Took him for seven large that night on a bad bet.
Richard Wright was a code word & a mountain range
& a treble clef. I tell you, Richard Wright could fly!

Old heads say they saw him soar in circa late summer
of '59, sitting cross-legged & singing gospel
from the saddled back of an inner-city tortoise.

Richard Wright taught us how to forfeit.
Richard Wright was a steel-driving man.
Richard Wright outlived everything he ever built.

Richard Wright built the White House.
Hammered each nail into place
with his unadorned hands.

Richard Wright was a monument
all by himself. Richard Wright
was a soda can.

Retire whom? I am the unrestrained fleet
of bone that cancels your shame.
The deadliest squadron of five.
Every time this cannonball dives
into airborne thrust it is always
all over, playboy,
& don't you forget it.

Before pen or pot handle
unlearned you the splendor of blood,
I taught bully's breath to bow,
plowed your father's truancy
into that punk's front teeth
like a rust
darting through snow.

C'mon, now.
Who knows you better
than the black of your hand?

Who held you down
when the whole world went
spaghetti western & you
were six bullets short of a coffin's kiss?

Exactly.

Now look at you.
All emotional,
as if there was ever a choice.

As if all this glory
was up for discussion.

Unnatural nasty.
Inimitable mirror.
Latchkey kid lyric
condition of possibility
light-years before blocksong
seep in or creep over crooked
pew of glass teeth. Both mainstream
science & neighborhood lore afford me
life after aftermath is afterthought. I am always
forefront of family fight, why Ma sling Pop
side-eye over supper five nights out of seven
on a good week. I put the pest in pestilence.
The silence too. My nondescript haunting
be quiet as a fist & damn near immortal.
& ain't that some kind of perverse
irony: our ubiquity in this
crumbling kitchenette,
the sheer pluck
of indestructible
vermin eons older
than the human
eye, its irrelevant
contempt?

In the first instance, we might say the word *stupid* is a tiger the black child does or does not outrun from birth. The data bears this out, though we can linger with the following image if we want our claim to be death-proof: by the time Ms. Hollinger told my father I would never function in a classroom, I held as many years as a handgun's worth of ammo in my body. The term *function* is of singular import here. Not only as an allusion to the mechanical—which is to say, grade school as the Industrial Revolution's unclaimed offspring— but also its broader implications for the social field: the function as a math problem involving one, two, as many unknowns as you can fit into a fist. Still, it was clear that I was not what most would call *stupid*, though there was certainly something *stupid-esque* about my refusal of Ms. Hollinger's most basic orders: coloring when it was time for naps, my index finger sketching narwhals onto the air as she droned over ABC's: "Two things are infinite: the universe and human stupidity; but I am not so certain about the universe." That's Einstein. Seriously. Which leads me to believe that what Ms. Hollinger intended was not as vile or violent as it first seemed. Perhaps what she meant to say was not so apocalyptic at all, but her attempt at gluing language to the ineffable, not unlike how we give human names to tropical storms, or look at the stars and say the word *stars*, like our mouths are big enough to capture all of the light at once.

I take my cue from the blizzard
making a name for itself outside
the café window: give myself away
in shards. First, each hour spent
on the threshing floor, so hungry
for the force of the Lord
there were days I dared not move, poring
over ancient law until the walls bled.
Then, the flashing image of Princeton
in 1856, every slave a young man brings
to campus dressed in black, an extra pair
of hands to mend the trousers, or brush
his hair before bed. Then my father scaling
the side of our house with no ladder, too poor
to call the locksmith. Then the blond man
on the A train last month, his broken nose turning
each fist into a bolt of red silk. Then my father again,
but smaller this time. This time no one pities him.
He is prettier than everyone else on the elevator.
My mother still jokes about catching him catching
himself in the switchboard's reflection, as if an Afroed
Narcissus seconds before the fall, all thirty-two teeth
shining bright as Lucifer's waistcoat.

VARIATION ON THE FATHER AS NARCISSUS[1]

---

[1] *Listen. What I mean to say is, I am not very much like him at all. I do not adorn myself with the bones of birds for fear of drowning. I will not eat any animal that can solve a puzzle, or suckles its young. I am not trying to make myself beautiful for you. I am not a cadaver yet.*

FRESH

I wasn't being fresh when I told
my father his word was good
as fish grease in a heatless house

as far as Mama or I was concerned.
So I don't know what cut him clean,
what tensed each arm

or gave his precious temper
flight. I never say the right
thing. All my rebuttals land

awkwardly, as if
they started dying
on the way down.

Back in his day Pop was the freshest dude this side of the BK Bridge, &
the runner-up wasn't close enough to make out the color of his socks, you
dig? He used to rock these three-piece polyester suits that made him look
like a redwood come alive just to stunt. Story goes, Mama saw him in a
club downtown & his rendition of the hustle was so smooth she got stuck
in his glow for like a whole minute before the bridge of the song gave her
body back to itself. Or maybe it was the other way. Maybe Mama was
both the dance floor & the light that called it forth. Maybe Pop never
danced, but was so lovely Mama released her hold on the room for like
three or four whole minutes, just to show the charmer how to move as if
the heat was its own currency: the kind of danger you could pay rent with.

The freshest memory I have
of my father takes place
in an IHOP in Washington
Heights & he is eating eggs,
describing my diction
as if it were on display,
floating in a bulletproof box:
The way all those words
come out of your head, man.
It's amazing. It's like a book
or something.

The boxing gym was across the street.
Its blue floor was soft and dull.
The coach was kind enough.
His name was Ralph. His shirt was clean
and nonspecific, the inverse of my moth-worn
Syracuse lacrosse sweatshirt.
The first class would be free.
The gym was across the street.
From my apartment, I mean.
The five-floor walk-up full of art
students and great-aunts
with names that ring like elegies.
I live next door to a Planet
Fitness full of shiny people.
My arms are smooth as shellfish.
There is no time like the present to pray
for difference. This is how the hunted persist.

◆

Christina and her friends threw me
up against the fence, held me
like a portrait in a museum boasting
free admission for students under the age
of ten. The chain-link made latticework
of my unremarkable back. Thankfully,
no archaeological evidence of this
remains. When I fell to the ground,
the other children circled me like a plague.
Humor was no reliable salvation:

Eight on one can't be that much fun for any of us,
am I right? The jury returned in a flash,
a unanimous decision to shake up the show
-off. From the blue floor of our newly
renovated playground, Ian's face
was all I could recognize. I charged
at him like a mother walrus darting
through the deep. Ian fell as a tooth
might, his space in the phalanx
suddenly filled only by my supple ghost.

◆

My dad could beat up anybody
else's dad. I knew this largely through folklore
he spun from the day of my birth
until first signs that his jet-black
curls would soon settle into winter.
In my unkempt head, the transition
from Jim Crow to Vietnam was clean
as blood could ever be, two battlefields
branding him iconic, unkillable.
He chased Tamara's ex-boyfriend
through an entire apartment complex
with no break for breath or drink. Punched a hole
in a wall after a parent-teacher conference
ended with the indictment of his favorite son.
His third second chance. The youngest one.
The loyal prodigy, destined never to crystallize
into proper mirror, never master the alchemy

of knuckle blooming into broken nose,
jaw left hanging like a half pendulum,
red asymmetry shaming a stranger's face.

In a sense, you are the valve
through which the game's hard
beauty finds its most fitting
point of egress. You who turn fist
swing & broken limbs into box scores,
boost a benchwarmer's prayer
with every figure you sketch
in that green book you keep, always,
flush to your chest, as if a secret
weakness or tale of a simpler time
long since gone rogue. Let popular culture
have its jokes, its jockstraps & sweaty socks
thrown like gossip across the locker room, the business
end landing squarely on your face each time.
What do they know of the math you bend
to make scholarships materialize, the scores
of glistening boys you daily break free?
It is a kind of love, I think, your tireless glare
trailing every shot, the waltz of iron
& wood you give back to the page, all those
small, black gifts exploding into song.

FAMILY REUNION

for Tariq

The question quarantines.
My cousin's usual talk
of anime & first apartments
& Kiana Thomas's flawless
hips has long ceased, faded
like ghost kisses into the tepid
night. I try & fail at least four times
to make this into a conversation
about wonder, do my best
to make the doubt sound pretty:
But who did Jesus think he was,
exemplar or experimentalist?
I watch the chariot wheels
spinning in his eyes turn over & over.
This is the longest we have spoken
in ten years, the sword now so deep
I could not retrieve it without killing us both.

It all started with the Hammond B-3
electric organ I saw at the thrift store
on 234th Street around two in the afternoon,

while everyone else was in a seminar
on Hegel, feigning agreement.
I captured the image of the holy

device on my new phone, sent it off
to all my fellow former saints.
Within minutes, we had a space

and a plan. Our agnostic church
would meet in my apartment every
other week, just the three of us

on beanbags and half-broken
chairs, belting the hymns our mothers
sewed into our hands.

For a name, Jamall suggests *First
Humanist Church of Washington Heights*,
but Jeremy finds that rather dull

& I don't disagree strongly enough,
so we toss out a few more, most
involving Brooks, Baraka, Hughes,

three or four other poets who called God
lonely—not as insult, but as
a critique of perfection, a guess

at what sovereignty does
to one's social life—before
settling on *Praise House*,

a unanimous choice once
I pulled up the photo of a man
old enough to have lived

when it was illegal to do
what we do for a living now,
his arms akimbo, standing

in front of an oat-white lean-to,
the name of our new sanctuary
typeset across the side.

Though I do not know if this building bore
any relation to what our parents
would call *sacred*, if those living

at the borders of this black
& white still did anything more
than walk into a splintering box

and cry the hours into their hands,
I can say, without certainty
or shame, that we have come

here with no aim higher than that
kind of blood & saltwater prayer.
As all those who went before,

we know God is an event,
that the spirit will not fall
if the music ain't right. Thus,

gathered in the name of what
gathers us, we lose our selves
in spite of our dialectical

minds, invite the groove
to take us in, take us
higher, alight.

All my favorite singers sound like modems.
I intend this to be read as a loving observation
the same way an aging mechanic lifts the engine
from the torso of his Cutlass Supreme

& sends it off to become someone else's future.
Which is to say, coolly, I know what time it is.
All my favorite singers sample dead legends
& let the spirit speak in HD:

Heathen's Desire, Holy Diffraction—
the only difference worth noting
is whether you want your body
to be something it is not or someplace

it has never been when the synth-laden outro
begins. Whether you do or do not believe
that freaky cyborgs are indeed among us
when the bass kicks you upside the knees

like a little brother testing his legs, his luck,
your love. All my favorite singers tend to refrain
from using terms like *love* unironically,
which could be read as a way of distancing

what we came here for or what we built
this petulant hunger from. Zapp & Roger
hum *compuuuter luuuuuuv* & I don't
imagine another person on the end

of another screen, blowing emoji kisses at me
from across the distance, but a glowing Xbox
One, my first iPhone, this smooth black alphabet
full of wires & light, lying to my escapist

heart, daring this flesh to be its own
system of stars & gas giants, unfurling
into the slick ether like cellophane, like everywhere
& nowhere I have ever wanted to be.

IN DEFENSE OF DMX

No one knows Ella Fitzgerald
was raised in Yonkers,

which probably makes you
the most famous person

to ever hail from Yonkers & most days
I'm pretty cool with this gap in the archive

if only because of that part in the *Grand Champ* intro
where your homeboy says, *Fact of the matter is, I trust dogs*

more than I trust humans & I feel pretty
much the same way only

you should switch out dogs
for written agreements

or Apple products in my case.
I love how you love the ostensible

subhuman. How you praise even
the unworthy muse. How even

your prayers sound like fighting, which
reminds me of my mother & her Bapticostal

ilk, the way they would bless the air
when kin grew sick or shut in, every line

of holy petition invisible & yet swinging,
this knot of bodies locked to Mama's tone.

You are churchy too, but in a dangerous way
& I respect that. Such multiplicity is no doubt born

of your nameless hometown & no friends to speak
about such things with, the lack of empathy for boys

from yet-unpopular wars. When strangers ask
where I'm from, I either lie (some nonsense

about a BX birthright by maternal bloodline)
or invoke your name to laminate my hood credentials.

It never works as intended,
but I don't blame you.

Our voices occupy different spaces
on the *Trust, You Don't Want No Problems*

spectrum, & I usually follow up any claim
to our home, our beloved, mutual shame

by mentioning the Ovidian qualities
of your more recent work & you know

how it is, Earl. You know nothing beautiful
comes from where we come from.

So when I talk about you like that,
I think it confuses people.

Older even than sport itself is this sex
of soul & pelt, this leap & sway to set
a crowd aflame. By all means, play
on, fanciful false animal snout
slick with fang & teenage gall,
strut till the fur feels like a spare
body you could claim as chain
mail, as buffer, as college essay
fodder par excellence if it weren't
for all the other awesome stuff
you do when the suit is left
hanging like a salted hide
in your gym locker, days when you
are just a scholarship with teeth who
writes what you cannot name
but know is there, the way your father
knows each bone in his back
is there, by the pain that cracks the quiet,
the spell your skin casts over every classroom
you enter. On principle, the dancing
routine complicates things but you, sir,
are distinctly postmodern
in your ideas about race
& performance though you
do not yet know the word *postmodern*
do not yet know the word *performance*
as anything other than what happens when
halftime hits & the latest radio fare
slinks through the speakers

as if a hunter made entirely of oil
& it is time to feed
the people what
they came here for.

is where I learned to brandish the black like a club,
you know, like a blunt object, or cobalt flashes of strobe
dotting damp walls after dusk drops the dark motion
our modern world can't hold. There's a process
by which bodies blend in, or don't, or die, or roll on
past the siren's glow so as not to subpoena the grave.
Mama never said surviving this flesh was a kind
of perverse science, but I've seen the tape,
felt the metal close & lock around my wrists, witnessed
bone bisected by choke hold. A crow turns crimson
against the windshield & who would dare mourn
such clean transition, the hazard of not knowing
you are the wrong kind of alive. But enough
about extinction. Entire towns mad with grief, whole
modes of dreaming gone the way of life before lyric,
all faded into amber & archive, all dead as the VCR,
all buried below the surface where nothing breaks, bleeds.

When I was four, an elderly white woman bought my elementary school while I was still going to school inside of it. Tore the building down. Now, it's a parking lot.

HOME FORCE: PRESUMPTION OF DEATH

erasure of Florida Statute 776.013

person is presumed to have a self or body.
        person gains unlawful dwelling, or occupies

against will. personhood does not apply
        if the son against whom force is used

has no lawful owner or title to protect.
        violence against the child is wise.

official duties: the officer identifies
        any applicable reason. so tempting

to attack, retreat, stand and meet
        force with dead. it is necessary

to prevent the body, harm
        him, sing *get over it.*

TENACIOUS ELEGY: INSURGENT LIFE IN THE ERA OF TRIAL BY GUNFIRE WITH A LINE FROM SYLVIA WYNTER

Keywords: kin, walking, home, store, cop, child, mother, gone, shots, badge, blue, no, no, no, no

Abstract:

To be sure, our moment demands a song. Yet the question of how one responds at the level of lyric to the relentless event that operates under the sign of the public lynching—this wound that doubles as the primary ghost of black social life in the modern era; that is, the transformation of a friend's life into figures, fictions, ink almost stoic against the page, details that bloom & fade at the speed of an eye's aversion—remains open: a dehiscence, howling. What to do with all of the faces? Or the trembling they leave in their wake, the toy guns & playdates we take from the children? How does one marshal imagery in the name of such a cause, asserting flora where doom has staked its ground, its claim to the very language an author might wield to smith a vision worth its weight in blood? In an effort to wrestle with these questions & others until a proper ceremony can be found, this poem is interested in enacting the world it yearns for, & begins with the image of its speaker on the second day of teaching his daughter to fly a two-wheeler, the machine's yellow steel like a thrush of finches shredding the natural sky, our speaker thinking for the first time in weeks that he might not be dead in every meaningful sense of the term, that he has in fact never felt so full, never felt this much like the sea unbuckling its mouth that all those old drowned saints might walk.

ANTHROPOPHOBIA

Before people question why the contact was made in the first place, they
should understand that Myers was no angel. . . . This is not a victim;
this is a victim-maker. This is not a martyr.

—JEFF ROORDA, BUSINESS MANAGER
OF THE ST. LOUIS POLICE UNION

The steel blue ghost standing
at the podium says VonDerrit Myers
was no angel & all I can hear is

the boy was a human boy. The boy
had a best friend & 206 bones. The boy
had a name that God didn't give him.

When he died, he did not bleed
starlight or gold. He was not half-bird.
The gun spoke, & no flaxen wing shot

from each shoulder, as if to carry him beyond
the bullet's swift assignment. No, the boy
was not a pillar of white smoke bright

enough to break a nonbeliever, make a penitent
fall prostrate, heaving, heavy with contrition, but
let me be clear: we are simply running out

of ways to shame the dead. How else to say
that we are guilty & yet unburied? How else
to erase him, if we cannot feign omnipotence,

56

lay claim to the sky, excise heaven,
take aim at the boy just one more
time while everyone watches?

Are you a land inside the body? Or an elsewhere
the body collapses, where it goes to prune

the imagination, that thick orchard of lights? Are you
an especially stern vice principal, curing the hallway

of chatter? Is there a way back to between
your borders yet unrecorded, a path without maps

or meds? Is there a language beyond language,
that I might describe what comes before the stillness,

the staring upward for hours that pass like punches
to the inside of the head? This is the most lonesome anguish,

I think, though any such distinction is blurry at best, counter
-productive even, given the nature of our moments together,

how solace, a mangy fox, always slips from presence
to memory without leaving a note, not even to say

I miss the way your breath comes & goes.

One has to consider the material
conditions that produced this fate
-ful moment. A scatterplot of men slain
by jawbone. Violence as a kind of boomerang. Battle cries
at first sight of sun, the stretched bow
of these impossible arms, all that foreign blood
making magenta planets in the sand. Her beauty.
Enough gold to feed a family thrice over
if she budgets it right.

The most expedient option here
is to make this all about Delilah. Her easy
scissors. The vile ways of women lovely enough
to make you dry up the moat, damn the armor for scraps,
open the heart for new business, et cetera, et cetera.

But what about my player card?
The empty bed she could never bet on? What of the calls
from her countrymen, or their hungry gods, or the comeuppance
of a thousand boys left kinless by the same hands that held
her sleeping body like a lyre, built our kitchen table from scratch,
stroked her faithful, moonless hair every night
for minutes on end all because she once said
that it helped with the insomnia?

And maybe no one's happy,
I think to myself, usually during
the plane ride home or as I read dead French
philosophers on the couch,

only a child's height away
from my girlfriend, who, for real
for real, is a Platonic ideal in her own
right, all any reasonable citizen

of desire might dare
to imagine in these times
of breakup over text message
& earnest tweets left

unanswered for days. We fit
like the grooves on a bullet.
We both love Rilke & want
children & think furniture

design is pretty important.
Three months into our tour
of the human condition,
I dropped half my rent

on a Corinthian leather sofa
because it sounded cool
& she didn't eat anything
with preservatives in it,

so I figured, *No biggie.*
This is what all
functioning adults do. They lie
expensively. They lie

awake. They lie
on their side, eyes ajar,
lover dreaming of cormorants
right next to them, counting

the minutes until even this bows
to the sovereignty of rot. Beloved,
if I came from anything unworthy
of shame, I would say so. I wouldn't

brood across the country this way.
If I knew how to stop calling
your presence pity,
my therapist's couch would grow cold

as a slaughterhouse.
And is that what you want?
To break such a flawless routine?
To stop screaming at typewriters, expecting rain?

ON FLESH

I ran from it and was still in it.

—FRED MOTEN

Not the body,
but its bad
alibi. Its black
& blueprint.

Whole summers spent
at Messiah Baptist gave me
a hundred ways to kill the creature
that lived in & as my skin.

Saint Paul had a whole thornbush
in his. Whether this was metonym
or mere approximation of the shape
& texture of a wound too florid

to forgo mentioning, I was never quite sure.
But what is sureness to the shoreless?
When certain certainties fade
& every part of you poses

itself as open question to a world
it knew best through the lens of legend
(myth & maps & dead men with one name)
how do you reframe the body's conversation

with itself or other selves? & where is
the self these days? & what is the body
but a bag of blood? & what is love
but an excuse to melt into mad, wet math?

& who can stomach the math of meat?
What does the animal have or not have
that makes its body not a body, its death not death
as-such as Heidegger or a devout Heideggerian

might say? Who is to say where
outside begins & flesh ends? Perhaps we
are all just webs of blue information
intersecting, collapsing across strata

& calling it something else,
something other than entropy
or decay, a turf war with time.
So many names for breaking into this life

at angles unplanned & unknowable. It's true.
There is much to be praised in this house
of lightning & dust, this sloppy armor
we yearn to move more beautifully in.

Every time I attempt what I'm attempting
right now, it ends up as some sad lyric
about diagnosis & that sounds like

the one kind of violence I don't have
a pretty name for. In advance, I don't know
if this poem will bring the problem onstage

& then pretend it went away to college. I don't know
if there is any way around the problem itself,
which is that I can only call something love

if it comes packaged in language I can feel
the weight of & my brother doesn't always
look at me when I visit the house. Sometimes

he walks in & sits on the couch & watches
TV while I'm watching TV & our shared
thereness is a prize. Sometimes he asks

about me when I'm gone
& no one else ever does that.
Levi is my brother's name

& I wrote a poem
about him once
& it wasn't about him

as much as how fear stalks me
like an inheritance, how I fear
for him with all of my love,

how I know the world
like I know the names
of famous poets & the world

has claws, Levi. When you were born,
I ran back & forth across Auntie's
apartment until the floorboards complained

& I am still like that. I am still more proud
than I am brave & you are still the great joy of
our rugged hometown, an outlaw all the same.

Please, excuse my shadow. I can't
stop leaving. I don't know how
to name what I don't know

well enough to render
in a single sitting. Every poem
about us seems an impossible labor,

like forgetting the face
of the sea, or trying to find
a more perfect name for water.

which is neither misery
nor melancholy per se,
but the way anything buried
aspires. How blackness becomes
a bladed pendulum swaying between
am I not a man & a brother
& meat. How it dips
into the position
of the unthought,
then out. Trust me.
Foucault isn't
helpful here. I am after
what comes when the law leaves
a dream gutted. The space
between a plea & *please*.
A mother marching in the name
of another woman's dead children.
Not the anguish she carries alongside
her as if it were a whole, separate person,
but the very fact of her feet
addressing the pavement,
the oatmeal she warmed in the microwave
that morning, sugar & milk
& blueberries blending in a white bowl
as she reads the paper, taken aback
only by the number of bullets
they poured like a sermon into him.
How despair kills: too slow to cut
the music from a horn, or set
my nephew's laughter to dim.

I am dying, yes, but I am not the marrow
in a beloved's memory just yet.
Who can be alive today
& not study grief?
There are bodies everywhere,
but also that flock of cardinals
making the sky look patriotic.

As you are both Malcolm's
shadow & the black unknown
he died defending, I praise

your untold potential, the possible
worlds you hold within your body's
bladed frame. I love how you stand

in exultation, arms raised
to welcome the rain, the bolt,
whatever drops from the sky's slick shelf

without warning, as all plagues
do. Miracles too. & bombs that fall
from planes which hold men with eyes

aimed through long glass tubes. Tubes
that make a civilian's life look small.
Small enough to smoke. X marks the cross

-hairs, & the home an explosion turns to blur.
X marks the box on the form that bought
the bombs, paid the triggerman, sent

the senator's son off to school
without a drop of blood to temper
his smile, stain leather

boots, mar the occasion.
X: every algorithm's heart
-beat, how any & all adjacent

quantities bloom. A kiss.
How a signature knows
where to begin its looping

dance. Two hands balled
into fists, crossed
at the wrist, repping

the borough that gave
us B-boys, the Yankees,
my mother's left

hook, swift enough
to knock any living
thing off its feet

like a cartoon villain
bested by banana peel
or spilled oil, his eyes

now two black x's,
denoting absence.
The wrong answer

on a test. How
my great-great-
grandfather,

who could not read,
signed his name,
as if an homage

to his own opacity,
as if to say, *I contain
the unthinkable*, or, *I abstain.*

PREFACE TO A TWENTY-VOLUME REGICIDE NOTE

after Krista Franklin after Amiri Baraka

Lately, I've become accustomed to the way
each newly dead face flashes like a crushed fire

-work across the screen. The red mass
of each name. How each name settles,

a fistful of ash at the back of the throat.
I don't hope for cease-fire much, if you

must know. I don't pray for rain.
On a good day, I honor the war

by calling it war. I sing
along with the hook. I sing

every nigga is a star
& don't mean dead

things shine too. For shame,
my six-year-old nephew dreams

of a life indebted to invention,
his first prototype a blade

-thin suit to help the human body move
faster. For a muse, he claims nothing

more than the implicit sweetness of speed,
but I know his best heart, how he longs

for cousins to grow gray as an alloy alongside.
I think him a prophet. I think of the fire.

I think of the drones with pictures of first wives
in their wallets, their bad teeth, middle names,

401(k)s for when all of the blood dries. I think
of the badge & see children running,

children laughing, children cradled
in smoke all at the exact same time.

On a good day, I think *die die die*
& don't know where to aim

the hex, who to hunt down or cut
a deal with, some armistice

without end, a certain commitment
to infinitude built right into the fine

print, in an unexpected turn.
I don't want any more words

that heal. I want a language for being
born underground, gravestone quarried

the moment you arrive. I want explosions
or else a fresh cosmos. I want the fang

-white king splayed
against a throne of bones

I see in all my new dreams
gone. Spare me any coalition

that does not require blood.
Give me time to think & a hope

-less cause. Give me lethal
equipment. Give me the names

of the slain. Say each name
like benediction. Ask,

Who will claim this flesh?
Expect the quiet.

Expect the flood.

JOHN ASHBERY
Selected Poems
Self-Portrait in a Convex
   Mirror

PAUL BEATTY
Joker, Joker, Deuce

JOSHUA BENNETT
The Sobbing School

TED BERRIGAN
The Sonnets

LAUREN BERRY
The Lifting Dress

PHILIP BOOTH
Lifelines: Selected Poems
   1950–1999

JULIANNE BUCHSBAUM
The Apothecary's Heir

JIM CARROLL
Fear of Dreaming:
   The Selected Poems
Living at the Movies
Void of Course

ALISON HAWTHORNE DEMING
Genius Loci
Rope
Stairway to Heaven

CARL DENNIS
Another Reason
Callings
New and Selected Poems
   1974–2004
Practical Gods
Ranking the Wishes
Unknown Friends

DIANE DI PRIMA
Loba

STUART DISCHELL
Dig Safe

STEPHEN DOBYNS
Velocities: New and Selected
   Poems: 1966–1992

EDWARD DORN
Way More West

ROGER FANNING
The Middle Ages

ADAM FOULDS
The Broken Word

CARRIE FOUNTAIN
Burn Lake
Instant Winner

AMY GERSTLER
Crown of Weeds
Dearest Creature
Ghost Girl
Medicine
Nerve Storm
Scattered at Sea

EUGENE GLORIA
Drivers at the Short-Time Motel
Hoodlum Birds
My Favorite Warlord

DEBORA GREGER
By Herself
Desert Fathers, Uranium Daughters
God
Men, Women, and Ghosts
Western Art

TERRANCE HAYES
Hip Logic
How to Be Drawn
Lighthead
Wind in a Box

NATHAN HOKS
The Narrow Circle

ROBERT HUNTER
Sentinel and Other Poems

MARY KARR
Viper Rum

JACK KEROUAC
Book of Blues
Book of Haikus
Book of Sketches

JOANNA KLINK
Circadian
Excerpts from a Secret Prophecy
Raptus

JOANNE KYGER
As Ever: Selected Poems

ANN LAUTERBACH
Hum
If in Time: Selected Poems,
   1975–2000
On a Stair
Or to Begin Again
Under the Sign

CORINNE LEE
Plenty

PHILLIS LEVIN
May Day
Mercury
Mr. Memory & Other Poems

PATRICIA LOCKWOOD
Motherland Fatherland
   Homelandsexuals

WILLIAM LOGAN
Macbeth in Venice
Madame X
Strange Flesh
The Whispering Gallery

ADRIAN MATEJKA
The Big Smoke
Mixology

MICHAEL MCCLURE
Huge Dreams: San Francisco
   and Beat Poems

ROSE MCLARNEY
Its Day Being Gone

DAVID MELTZER
David's Copy: The Selected
   Poems of David Meltzer

ROBERT MORGAN
Dark Energy
Terroir

CAROL MUSKE-DUKES
An Octave above Thunder
Red Trousseau
Twin Cities

ALICE NOTLEY
Certain Magical Acts
Culture of One
The Descent of Alette
Disobedience
In the Pines
Mysteries of Small Houses

WILLIE PERDOMO
The Essential Hits of Shorty
   Bon Bon

LIA PURPURA
It Shouldn't Have Been Beautiful

LAWRENCE RAAB
The History of Forgetting
Visible Signs: New and Selected
   Poems

BARBARA RAS
The Last Skin
One Hidden Stuff

MICHAEL ROBBINS
Alien vs. Predator
The Second Sex

PATTIANN ROGERS
Generations
Holy Heathen Rhapsody
Wayfare

ROBYN SCHIFF
A Woman of Property

WILLIAM STOBB
Absentia
Nervous Systems

TRYFON TOLIDES
An Almost Pure Empty Walking

SARAH VAP
Viability

ANNE WALDMAN
Gossamurmur
Kill or Cure
Manatee/Humanity
Structure of the World Compared
   to a Bubble

JAMES WELCH
Riding the Earthboy 40

PHILIP WHALEN
Overtime: Selected Poems

ROBERT WRIGLEY
Anatomy of Melancholy and
   Other Poems
Beautiful Country
Earthly Meditations: New and
   Selected Poems
Lives of the Animals
Reign of Snakes

MARK YAKICH
The Importance of Peeling
   Potatoes in Ukraine
Unrelated Individuals Forming a
   Group Waiting to Cross